S0-AGX-077

Bmazo
$4.00

Songs of California

The
U.C.
Berkeley
Tradition

Compiled by the Cal Song Book Committee

Copyright © 2007 by The University of California, Berkeley, Class of 1957, an affiliate of the California Alumni Association, Inc.

The University of California, Berkeley has granted permission to the Class of 1957 to use images, symbols, and other materials incorporated in this book to the extent that the University owns or controls the same, including the reprinting thereof. Copyright permission has been granted from the other owners of other materials not under the control of the University so that they may be reproduced in this volume.

Cover and interior design: Margaret Copeland/Terragrafix

Printed by Medius Corp., Milpitas, CA

ISBN-13: 978-0-9799449-1-8

Library of Congress Cataloging-in-Publication Data in progress

---

Publisher's Note

On behalf of the University of California Class of 1957, we would like to extend our appreciation and thanks to the Song Book Committee which has done a great service to the University and our Class in producing this wonderful work. In particular, we would like to thank our classmate, John Vlahos, who identified the need for this publication, formed and led the Song Book Committee, did much of the creative work and was the editor of the book. Our Class enthusiastically adopted the proposal for this book when it was presented as the need for this work was immediately apparent, and Class members stepped up with donations to make the project a reality for which we are most grateful. We expect to donate the book in time to an appropriate campus organization which will perpetuate it and reprint it as necessary. Go Bears!

— *John A. Edginton*
Class of 1957 President

TABLE OF CONTENTS

DEDICATION

This new "Songs of California" is dedicated to Clinton R. "Brick" Morse, Ted E. Haley, Charles Mills Gayley, Harold Bingham and the other composers and lyricists named in these pages. Their creative energies and spirit began and perpetuated the heritage of Cal songs. It is also dedicated to Roschelle Paul Weiman and the late Professor Albert I. Elkus for their efforts in keeping that tradition alive during the dark days of World War II, providing the starting point and inspiration for this new and updated Cal song book.

ACKNOWLEDGMENTS

Publication of this book would not have been possible without the support and participation of a dedicated Song Book Committee: Robert O. Briggs, '51, Cal Band Director Emeritus; Howdy Brownson, '48, a member of the original U.C. Men's Octet; Robert Calonico, '76, Cal Band Director; Robert Commanday, M.A. '52, former Director of the Glee Club and Treble Clef, former *San Francisco Chronicle* Music Critic and founder of San Francisco Classical Voice; Robin Coulon, '67; Narsai David, '57; John Edginton, Class of 1957 Class President; Monroe Kanouse, '57; William Roberts, M.A. '63; Mark Sumner, Director of the University of California Choral Ensembles (UCCE); Carol Suveda, '81, UC Berkeley Student Musical Activities Department; Tom Watrous, '60; Carol Kavanagh Clarke, '60, Cal Spirit; and N.H. (Dan) Cheatham, '58, former Cal Band drum major. Thanks also to those members of the Committee in its original iteration over a decade ago: Michael Murakami, '66; the late Phillip Elwood, '45, former *San Francisco Examiner* Jazz Critic; Charles Gravenhorst, '83; Tony Pasqua, former Director of UCCE; the late Joe Willits, '48; and last, but not least, Roschelle Paul, '42, co-editor of the 1944 song book.

Special credit must be given to Carol Suveda and Robert Commanday for providing information to assist the editor's writing of the histories of some of the songs; to Carol Suveda, Margaret Copeland of Terragrafix, and Bill Roberts for their help in finding and assembling some of the photographs; to Monroe Kanouse for musical editing and supervision; to N.H. (Dan) Cheatham for his excellent input on the histories and Cal Band traditions; to Charles Gravenhorst, Baker Peeples, Musical Director of the San Francisco Lamplighters Musical Theater, and Michael Taylor for computer program transfer of the music and lyrics; and to Margaret Copeland for the graphic design of this song book. And special thanks to Robin Coulon for his always timely and energetic work in locating photographs and diligently following up on a myriad of research projects vital to the project, and to John Edginton, for his energy, support and encouragement, for his leadership in securing the support of the Class of 1957, for obtaining copyright clearances, and for his publication, legal and technical expertise. We also wish to thank Chancellor and Mrs. Robert Birgeneau for graciously permitting the use of the photograph in this song book of the late Professor Chiura Obata painting located in University House. And, finally, thanks to my wife, Martha Vlahos, for her diligent proofreading and thoughtful suggestions.

A tremendous debt of gratitude is owed to the Cal Class of 1957. When the idea of a new song book was presented to the Class Council shortly after the project was conceived, the Council quickly adopted it, and, through its Class gift fundraising, has underwritten the publication of this book. Without that support, this new song book would not have been possible.

The primary sources of the historical materials were Roschelle Paul's excellent and exhaustive 1945 Master of Arts thesis, "Song Tradition of the University of California at Berkeley," the Cal Band centennial book, *The Pride of California*, the Cal Band Website, the late S. Dan Brodie's book, *67 Years on the California Gridiron*, the University archives, and interviews with Roschelle Paul, Ned Flanders and Jonathan Elkus.

— *John Vlahos, Class of 1957,*
Editor and Chairman of the
Cal Song Book Committee

FOREWORD

Few, if any, universities have a college song tradition as rich as that of the University of California, Berkeley. In the early decades after the University's founding in 1868, the songs sung by students at the small, fledgling campus were merely popular songs of the day. But as faculty members were recruited from prestigious Eastern universities, they brought with them the college songs of those institutions, and the lyrics were quickly adapted to the new university. The 1890s saw the beginning of the creation of Cal's own college songs, and that tradition continued strongly through the 1930s. Cal songs were played by the Cal Band and sung by all the living groups, spirit groups, and the Glee Club, not only at athletic events but also at all University occasions and indeed on occasions and non-occasions of no particular consequence at all.

Then came World War II when most of the male students were in the armed forces. Many students on campus came from other colleges and universities and had no particular Cal allegiance. President Robert Gordon Sproul (himself a Cal Band drum major in his undergraduate days) became concerned about the possible disappearance of school spirit. He asked Roschelle Paul, Class of 1942 (now Roschelle Paul Weiman), Director of the Glee Club and Treble Clef and accompanist at various University functions, to find a way to preserve that spirit. Professor of Music Albert I. Elkus suggested to her a portable song book from which students could learn the Cal songs. This led to the creation of the 1944 *Songs of California*, edited by Ms. Paul and Professor Elkus, and aided by a song book committee under the auspices of the California Alumni Association. Gathering at noon by the Campanile, and later, as the crowds got bigger, on Faculty Glade, students learned the songs using the new song book.

While the tradition was carried on by the unflagging devotion of the Cal Band, as well as the Glee Club and Treble Clef, and successor student singing groups, the turbulent 1960s took their toll. Over time, it appeared that fewer and fewer students and alumni actually knew, sang or played these wonderful songs. In the 1990s, I became interested in the preservation of Cal's song heritage. I was chagrined to find that there had been no new comprehensive Cal song book since the 1944 version. That discovery was the motivation for the formation of a new committee to compile and publish a new song book.

This new *Songs of California* is intended, as was its 1944 predecessor, to preserve Cal's rich musical heritage and revitalize the singing and playing of these songs. It includes all the selections in the 1944 book, save the "St. Anne Hymn," the university hymn seldom sung by students. It also includes a number of the new ones written since the 1944 publication. And, since tradition is built upon history, the history of each of the songs has been provided.

So, to paraphrase, "Sing for California, for California through and through."

— John Vlahos, Class of 1957,
Editor and Chairman of the
Cal Song Book Committee

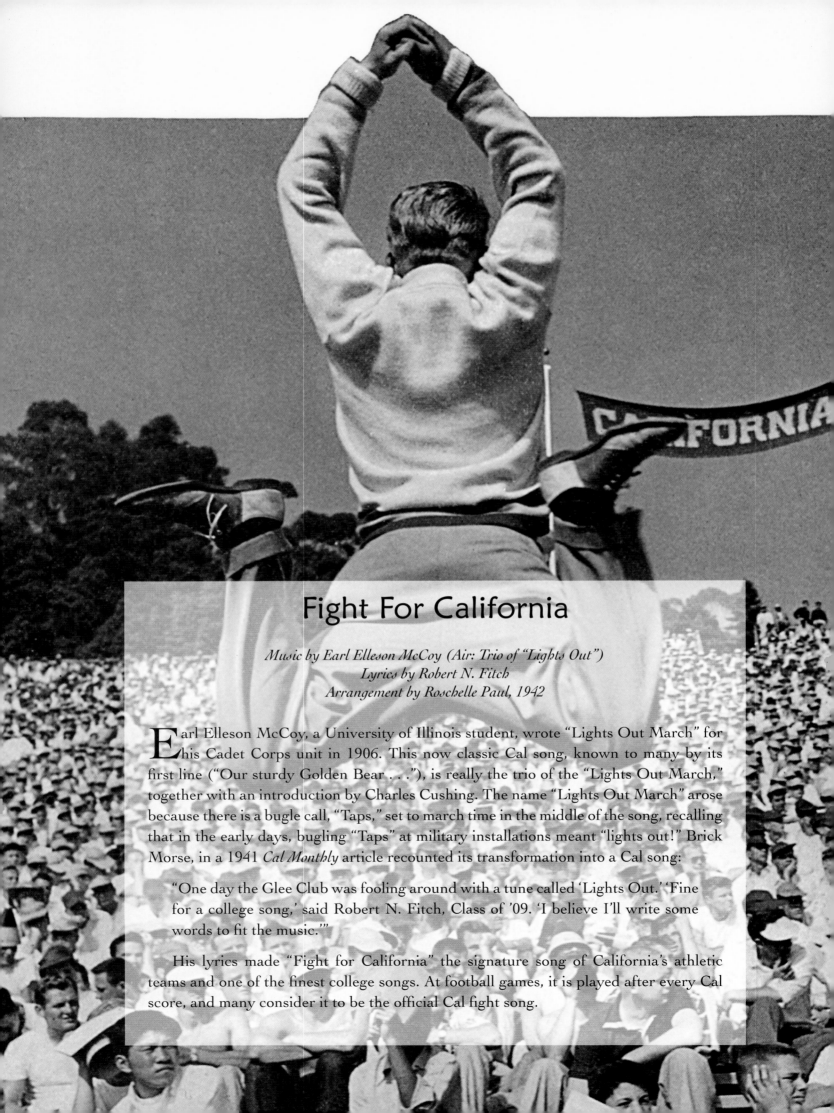

Fight For California

Music by Earl Elleson McCoy (Air: Trio of "Lights Out")
Lyrics by Robert N. Fitch
Arrangement by Roschelle Paul, 1942

Earl Elleson McCoy, a University of Illinois student, wrote "Lights Out March" for his Cadet Corps unit in 1906. This now classic Cal song, known to many by its first line ("Our sturdy Golden Bear . . ."), is really the trio of the "Lights Out March," together with an introduction by Charles Cushing. The name "Lights Out March" arose because there is a bugle call, "Taps," set to march time in the middle of the song, recalling that in the early days, bugling "Taps" at military installations meant "lights out!" Brick Morse, in a 1941 *Cal Monthly* article recounted its transformation into a Cal song:

> "One day the Glee Club was fooling around with a tune called 'Lights Out.' 'Fine for a college song,' said Robert N. Fitch, Class of '09. 'I believe I'll write some words to fit the music.'"

His lyrics made "Fight for California" the signature song of California's athletic teams and one of the finest college songs. At football games, it is played after every Cal score, and many consider it to be the official Cal fight song.

Fight For California

Lyrics by
ROBERT N. FITCH 1906

Air, Lights Out
By permission of Carl Fischer, Inc.,
copyright Proprietors

1. Our stur - dy Gold - en Bear, _____ Is
(2. Stal - warts) gird _____ ed for the fray, _____ Will

watch - ing from the skies, _____ Looks down _____ up -
strive _____ for vic - to - ry, _____ Their all _____ at

on our col - - ors fair, And guards us
Ma - ter's feet _____ wil lay. That brain and

from his lair._____ Our ban - - - ner
brawn will win the day. Our might - - - y

gold and blue,_____ The sym - bol on it
sons and true,_____ Will strive_____ for us a -

too,_____ Means } FIGHT for Cal - i - for - ni -
new,_____ And }

Fine

a, For Cal - i - for - nia through and through!_____

D.S. al Fine

2. Stal-warts

The 1895 track team whose exploits inspired "The Golden Bear"

The Golden Bear

Music from Air: "The Pope"
Lyrics by Charles Mills Gayley
Arrangement by Roschelle Paul, 1942

How did the Golden Bear become the mascot of Cal's athletic teams?

Credit the immediate popularity of this song when it was written in 1895. In that year, the track team, without trainer or coach, bereft of funds but determined to compete in eastern track meets against Princeton, Yale, Columbia and Chicago, managed to collect enough money from student body contributors to underwrite the trip. They took along a large blue banner with "a Golden Bear upon it too" for good luck. Displaying the banner at each meet, they were undefeated on the tour. When the tired but victorious team returned in the dead of night, they were welcomed by students and faculty at the Berkeley railroad station. As Professor Charles Mills Gayley (1858-1932) watched the scene, the words came to him.

Professor Gayley set his lyrics to the traditional air, "The Pope." An Englishman born in Shanghai, Gayley attended the University of Michigan, subsequently taught there and edited a "Yellow and Blue" song book. In 1889, he exchanged the "Yellow and Blue" of the University of Michigan for the "Blue and Gold" of the then small and little-known University of California, where he became and remained until 1923 a professor of English, and at one time Co-Administrator of the Presidency. He was a founder of The Golden Bear Honor Society, and "The Golden Bear" became the Society's official song.

One of the two original banners that inspired the song belongs to the University Archives and is on loan to the Hall of Fame Room at Memorial stadium. The whereabouts of the other banner are unknown.

The Golden Bear

Lyrics by
CHARLES MILLS GAYLEY

AIR: The Pope

2
And oh, that Bear's a glorious sight, glorious sight,
  A circling 'round the pole all night, pole all night,
And once you've seen him you're all right,
  You've seen our California Bear,
And once you've seen him you're all right,
  You've seen our California Bear.

3
Oh, he has a very patient air, patient air,
  He wears a Paderewski hair, 'rewski hair,
He's center rush in the heaven I swear,
  Our silent, sturdy, Golden Bear,
He's center rush in the heaven I swear,
  Our silent, sturdy, Golden Bear.

4
Oh, have you seen our banner blue, banner blue,
  The Golden Bear is on it too, on it too,
A Californian through and through,
  Our totem, he, our Golden Bear,
A Californian through and through,
  Our totem, he, our Golden Bear.

Men's Octet, winners of the 1998 National Competition of Collegiate A Cappella*

Sons Of California

Music by Clinton R. "Brick" Morse, 1896
Lyrics by Clinton R. "Brick" Morse, 1896
Arrangement by Roschelle Paul, 1942

Charles R. "Brick" Morse remains one of the greatest contributors to the Cal song tradition. A graduate of the Class of 1896 and a stellar athlete who lettered in every major sport, he directed the Glee Club and its predecessors from 1893 to 1926, taking them on a dozen tours throughout Europe, Canada and Alaska. Morse wrote not only "Sons of California," but also, in 1907, "Hail to California." They remain two of the most beloved Cal songs.

Morse claimed in a 1941 article in the *Cal Monthly* that he would "drum out" hundreds of Cal songs and then promptly forget them. Luckily, "Sons of California" and "Hail to California" were two that he wrote down, thus ensuring their survival.

Although the song was originally performed and sung quite slowly, a faster version played by the Cal Band in the late 1930s led to ever increasing popularity. By tradition, it is the second song played in the Band's football pre-game show.

* *The Men's Octet also won the competition, renamed The International Championship of Collegiate A Cappella, in 2000.*

Sons of California

Words and Music by
CLINTON R. MORSE '96

With feeling (not too slow)

We're sons of Cal - i - for - nia, A loy - al com - pa - ny, All____
We'll yell for Cal - i - for - nia, Dear moth - er of us all. We'll____
We're sons of Cal - i - for - nia, Fair mis - tress of the sea, And we'll

shout for Cal - i - for - ni - a, While we strive for vic - to - ry. All
fight for Cal - i - for - ni - a, Till the crim - son ban - ners fall, And
win for Cal - i - for - ni - a, Her____ glo - rious des - ti - ny. Then

a little faster   *broaden*   *in tempo*

sing the joy - ful cho - rus, As her col - ors we un - fold, Then hur -
raise the joy - ful cho - rus, As her col - ors we un - fold, For we'll
raise the joy - ful cho - rus, As her col - ors we un - fold, For we'll

rah for Cal - i - for - ni - a, And for the Blue___ and Gold.
win for Cal - i - for - ni - a, And for the Blue___ and Gold.
win for Cal - i - for - ni - a, And for the Blue___ and Gold.

Senior Women's Pilgrimage, 1921

California, We're For You

Music by Sidney K. Russell, 1919
Lyrics by Sidney K. Russell, 1919

"California, We're for You," a rousing song written by Sidney K. Russell has appeared in California song books since the 1921 edition. While it did not appear in other song sheets or football song pamphlets, nor was it mentioned in Blue & Gold annuals, it became part of the Glee Club's "New Medley" and has appeared in Cal Band recordings.

The Campanile, completed 1914

California, We're For You

Lyrics and Music by
SIDNEY K. RUSSELL 1919

Cal - i - for-nia's on the field to - day, Ev - 'ry
Sons of Cal - i - for - nia, brave and bold, Fight the

man is read - y for the fray; Gold and Blue means
bat - tle for the Blue and Gold. Brawn and brain are

tried and true___ And once a - gain you'll see___ That we are
all in vain___ Un - less our spir - it's there___ In ev - 'ry

March On, California

Music by Unknown (adapted from Ned Flanders' New Medley Glee Club song book)
Lyrics by Unknown (adapted from Ned Flanders' New Medley Glee Club song book)
Arrangement by Unknown

Unfortunately there is virtually no information available on the history or background of "March On, California," other than that it was adopted from the "New Medley" Glee Club song book, edited by Ned Flanders, 1940, senior manager of the Glee Club. The authors of the music and lyrics are unknown.

March On, California

Adapted from Ned Flander's
"New Medley"
Glee Club Song Book

Rather slow march

March on Cal - i - for - nia, de - fend thy an - cient fame.___ Fight

March on

once
on, Cal - i - for - nia, go out and win that game. Once

that game, once

more
more, once more may the glo - ry a - bove the fair un - fold, And

more

high in air the ban - ner of the Bear pro - claim the Blue___ and Gold.

Big "C"

Music by H.P. Williams, 1914
Lyrics by Norman Loyall McLaren, 1914
Arrangement by Roschelle Paul, 1942

In the first part of the 20th Century, it was customary on campus for the *Daily Cal* to conduct an annual song contest. "Big 'C'" was written to commemorate the big golden "C" symbol ("On our rugged eastern foothills . . . "). It won the 1913 contest over "The Stanford Jonah" (which was resubmitted and won the following year).

Many Cal students and alumni know this song by the first line of the second verse — "We are Sons of Califonia . . ." — thus causing some confusion with Brick Morse's "Sons of California." "Big 'C'" is traditionally the first song played by the Cal Band at football games as it marches onto the field from the North Tunnel of Memorial Stadium in its wedge formation.

The song also is the center of considerable controversy. At an All-University Weekend in the early 1960s, an arrangement of "Big 'C'"(made by the UCLA band director, himself a former Cal Bandsman and later involved with the Disneyland band) was played by the massed Cal, UCLA, UC Davis and UC Santa Barbara bands during the halftime of the Cal-UCLA football game. Thereafter, UCLA "adopted" the song over the continuing protests of the Cal Band director, Band members and students who objected both to the "adoption" of a Cal song and the "Hollywood" treatment of the arrangement. The Cal Band Director, the late James Berdahl, was incensed to the point of considering litigation until it was discovered in 1969 that the song, never having been copyrighted, was in the public domain. Nonetheless, when played by the UCLA band, it calls forth derisive shouts from Cal students (and alums with institutional memories), "Get your own song!"

15

Big "C"

Lyrics by
NORMAN LOYALL McLAREN 1914

Music by
H. P. WILLIAMS 1914

Cal - i-for - ni-a!

On our rug-ged East-ern Foot-hills, Stands our sym-bol clear and
We are sons of Cal - i - for - nia, Fight - ing for the Gold and

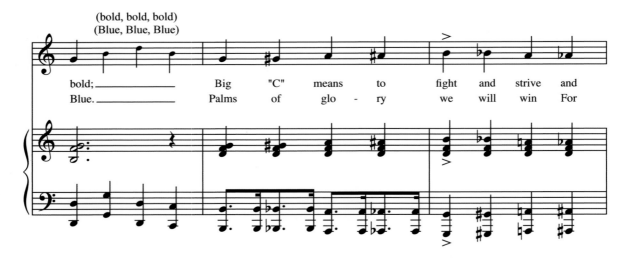

(bold, bold, bold)
(Blue, Blue, Blue)

bold;_____ Big "C" means to fight and strive and
Blue._____ Palms of glo - ry we will win For

win for Blue and Gold. / Al - ma Ma - ter true.

Gold - en Bear is e - ver / Stan - ford's men will soon be

watch - ing; / rout - ed

Day by day he prowls, / By our daz - zling "C",

And / And

when he hears the tread / when we sur - pen - tine,

Of low - ly Stan - ford red, / Their red will turn to green,

From his lair he fierce - ly / In our hour of vic - to -

1.

growls.

(Yell:) Gr - rr - rah, Gr - rr - rah, Gr - rr, — rr - rah!

D.C.

2.

ry

Cal Band March

Music by Jonathan Elkus, 1953
Lyrics by Robert Bramson, 1977, and Susan Mattson, 1981
Arrangement by Jonathan Elkus, 1953

"Cal Band March" was commissioned in 1978 by the Board of Directors of Tellefsen Hall (established by Cal Band Alumni as a dorm for Band Members) in memory of Cliff Tellefsen, a long-time ASUC employee and Band supporter who was the first person to be named an Honorary Member of the Band. The music was written by Jonathan Elkus, Student Director of the Band in 1952 and son of Professor Albert Elkus, the co-editor (with Roschelle Paul) of the revival 1944 Cal song book. Jonathan Elkus later served from 1993 to 2003 as director of the U.C. Davis Cal Aggie Marching Band. Shortly after the music was composed, the Band conducted a contest for the lyrics. The winners, Robert Bramson, '77, and Susan Mattson, '81, wrote one verse each. The song (actually the trio of the full "March") was little played after it was performed at the Band's 1980 Spring Show, but was revitalized in 1991 as part of the Band's pre-game show. The full "Cal Band March" was played again at the Band's 1992 Spring Show.

The original "Cadet Band," 1891

Cal Band, 1941

Cal Band, 2006

19

Commissioned by the Tellefsen Hall Board of Directors
in memory of Chris Tellefsen (1892-1975)

Cal Band March

Lyrics by
ROBERT BRAMSON 1977
and SUSAN MATTSON 1981

Music by
JONATHAN ELKUS 1953

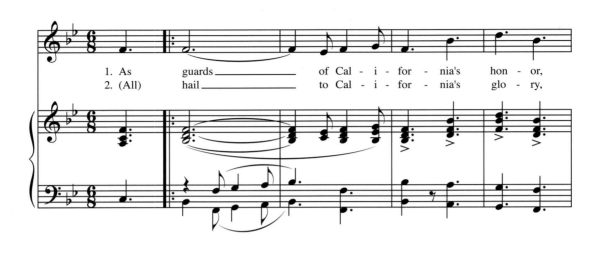

1. As guards _____ of Cal - i - for - nia's hon - or,
2. (All) hail _____ to Cal - i - for - nia's glo - ry,

we march _____ a - long, _____ And loyal _____
vic - tors _____ we rise, _____ And still, _____

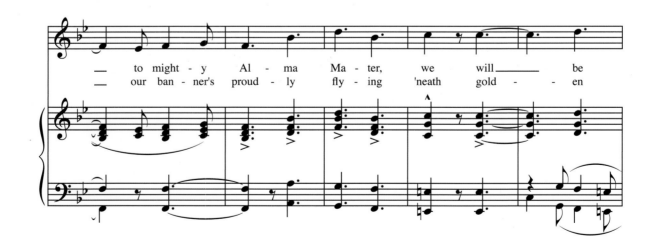

_____ to might - y Al - ma Ma - ter, we will _____ be
_____ our ban - ner's proud - ly fly - ing 'neath gold - - en

20

strong._____ For we know_____ a - bout her glo - rious
skies._____ March - ing on,_____ our dreams and bu - gles

fu - ture And we want to lead the way,_____ And when the
call - ing For our glo - rious des - ti - ny,_____ While all our

game's done, Cal - i - for - nia's Gold - en Bear has
heart's true, Car - ry forth the Gold and Blue through-

car - ried_____ the day._____ 2. All
out land_____ and "C."_____

1. 2.

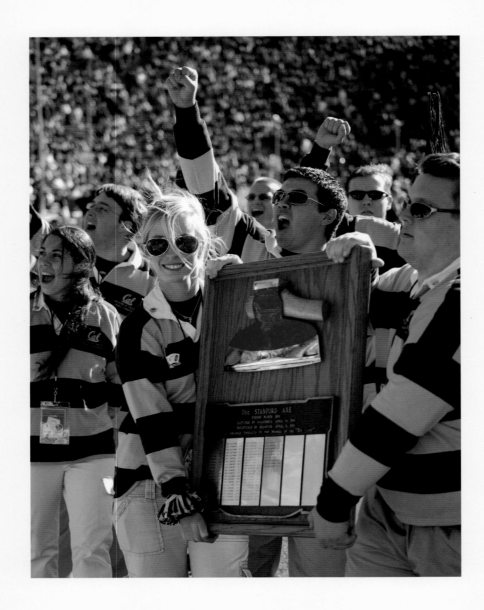

The Stanford Jonah

Music by Ted E. Haley, 1915
Lyrics by Ted E. Haley, 1915

Written in 1913 by Ted Haley, Class of 1915, "The Stanford Jonah" lost out to "Big 'C'" in the annual *Daily Cal* campus song contest that year, but was selected by the Rally Committee as the winner the following year after it was performed and popularized by the Glee Club. Haley learned to write songs from his father, a singer and actor who, under the name Billy Bray, wrote many popular songs in the 1880s.

There seems to be some controversy about the composer of the music. Brick Morse, in his October, 1941 article in the *California Monthly* attributed both music and lyrics to Haley, stating: "Ted Haley went to Europe with the Glee Club in 1914. Before we went, Ted wrote 'The Stanford Jonah' which we learned and sang on the trip." The author of the report on the Cal Band website, however, states that the tune appears to be unoriginal and that versions of the song may exist at Georgia Tech and the U.S. Naval Academy. He speculates that Georgia Tech may have acquired the tune from Cal after the 1929 Rose Bowl game between Cal and Georgia Tech. Whatever the source of the music, "The Stanford Jonah's" spirited rhythm and appropriate text vividly captures the pervasive Big Game excitement.

The Stanford Jonah

Lyrics and Music by
T. E. Haley 1915

Lively

When the train - ing days are done, And the big game's just be - gun, And there's mu - sic in the air; When our team runs on the field Stan - ford knows her fate is

sealed, For the Gold-en Bear has left his lair._____ When the

yells from lus-ty throats start to get-ting Stan-ford's goat, And the

root-ing sec-tion seems a howl-ing mob,_____ then you grab your hat and

shout, You let folks know you're a - bout, For you know that Stan-ford's

CHORUS

Jo - nah's on the job._____ So then it's up with the

Blue and Gold, Down with the Red, Cal - i - for - nia's

out for a vic - to - ry. We'll drop our bat - tle axe on Stan - ford's

head, When we meet her, our team will sure - ly beat her,

Down on the Stan - ford Farm there'll be no sound, When our

Os - ki rips through the air. Like our friend Mis - ter

Jo - nah, Stan - ford's team will be found In the tum - my of the

1.
Bear. _____ So then it's

2.
Bear. _____

Fight 'Em!

Music by I.B. Kornblum, 1917
Lyrics by H.E. Kowalski, 1916
Arrangement by Roschelle Paul, 1942

Card stunts at 1915 ersatz "Big Game" against Washington

The roughness that had developed in American football resulted in national controversy, but it was still a shock when, in March, 1905, Cal and Stanford agreed to drop football in favor of rugby. This was done despite changes in national football rules designed to make the game safer — legalization of the forward pass, shortening the game to two thirty-minute halves, and drawing lines the length of the field at five-yard intervals parallel to the sidelines to help officials determine the legality of the new forward pass under the then complicated rules. (The pattern thus created as these lengthwise lines crossed the sideline to sideline yardage marker lines resulted in the coining of the name "gridiron" for a football field.)

When the Cal-Stanford agreement expired in 1915, Cal's insistence on a rule making freshmen ineligible led to a breakdown in Cal-Stanford athletic competitions. So, in that year Cal looked north to the University of Washington, which had never abandoned football, for a new "Big Game" in 1915. Finally, in 1918, football games between Cal and Stanford resumed (along with a rugby game that year). Cal won the football game 67-0, but that game is not included in official Big Game records because of some confusion on the matter of eligibility.

Originally known as "Down From the North" but called "Fight 'Em" since at least the early 1920s, this song was written to commemorate the "Big Game" with Washington. According to "Brick" Morse: "We took I.B. Kornblum into the Glee Club not on account of his voice, but because he was a good instrumentalist. He rewarded us by writing the music to 'Fight 'Em.' It was very timely, for in 1915 our Big Game was with Washington, but our songs referred to Stanford. Kowalski's 'Down From the North' filled the bill admirably."

Fight 'Em!

Lyrics by
H. E. KOWALSKI, 1916

Music by
I. B. KORNBLUM, 1917

Gold - en Bear,_____ Wash - ing - ton's 'lev - en will

nev - er hold_____ the_ charge of our might - y Bear,_____

____ The team on the field is a line of steel_____ And_

ev - 'ry man is game,_____ When the strength of the

Blue and Gold they feel_____ Those North - men will be

tame._____ So, fight, fight, fight, fight, fight, fight,

fight, fight, FIGHT! for the Blue and the Gold_____ And our

team on the field will not bend, break or yield, For we'll fight like Big

"C" teams of old;_____ And ev - 'ry time they buck the line, We're sure the team will hold;_____ For vic - to - ry means fame for Cal - i - for - nia's name, So fight, fight, fight 'em Cal - i - for - nia!

Robert Commanday conducting the Glee Club, 1961

A Toast To California

Music by J. Murray Hunt, 1917
Lyrics by J. Murray Hunt, 1917
Arrangement by Robert Commanday

In 1956, J. Murray Hunt, 1917, inspired by a Glee Club-Treble Clef Alumni Reunion he attended, completed a song he had been working on — "A Toast to California." The Glee Club's Senior Men's Octet premiered the song at a Peninsula party, and it became part of the repertoire of the Glee Club, as well as the Cal Band. A new arrangement by Tony Pasqua, former director of the UC Alumni Chorus and the UC Men's and Women's Chorales, is now one of those ensembles' signature pieces.

A Toast to California

Arranged by
ROBERT COMMANDAY

Words and Music by
J. MURRAY HUNT '17

Hail To California

Music by Clinton R. "Brick" Morse, 1896
Lyrics by Clinton R. "Brick" Morse, 1896
Arrangement by Roschelle Paul, 1942

"Hail to California," the second of Brick Morse's great contributions to the Cal song legacy, was written in 1907. It has become a virtual second Alma Mater, joining "All Hail! Blue and Gold." Traditionally, "Hail to California" is sung before football and basketball games, and "All Hail" is sung after the game. In 1952, the California Club (created in 1934 by University President Robert Gordon Sproul to create statewide University spirit as more campuses were added to the system) adopted "Hail to California" as the statewide University hymn, but its major popularity remains in Berkeley. Some decry the fact that in some quarters, "Hail to California" has seemingly supplanted "All Hail! Blue and Gold" as the Cal Alma Mater. However, "All Hail" remains the official Alma Mater.

Hail to California

Words and Music by
CLINTON R. MORSE '96

With dignity

Hail to Cal - i - for - nia, Al - ma__ Ma - ter dear
Hail to Cal - i - for - nia, Queen in__ whom we're blest

Sing the joy - ful cho - rus Sound it__ far and near
Spread - ing light and good - ness O - ver__ all the West

Rally - ing 'round her ban - ner We shall nev - er fail_____
Fight - ing 'neath her stand - ard We shall sure pre - vail_____

Cal - i - for - nia Al - ma Ma - ter Hail! Hail! Hail!
Cal - i - for - nia Al - ma Ma - ter Hail! Hail! Hail!

California Marching Song

Music by Charles Hart
Lyrics by W.B. Garthwaite, 1918

With words by W.B. Garthwaite, a Cal alumnus, and music by Charles Hart, the "California Marching Song" was adapted from a 1927 San Francisco Bohemian Club Bohemian Grove play, "St. Francis of Assisi" by Irving Pichel and Charles Hart. Once used by the Glee Club as part of its New Medley (consisting of the following songs: "California, We're for You," "March On, California," "California Marching Song" and the "California Indian Song"), it is now traditionally played by the Cal Band as it exits Memorial Stadium, followed immediately by "One More River." The Band sometimes sings the song in four-part harmony, with accompaniment by solo baritone horn and sousaphone.

California Marching Song

Adapted from "St. Francis of Assisi"
Bohemian Club Grove Play by
Irving Pichel and Charles Hart, 1927

Music by
CHARLES HART

Words by
W. B. GARTHWAITE, '18

*By Permission of
The Bohemian Club,
San Francisco, California*

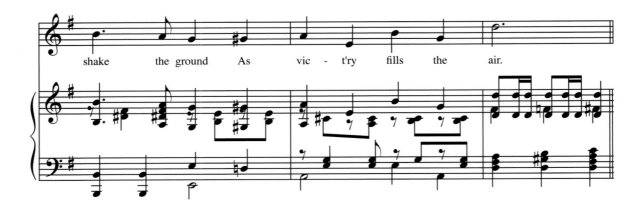

shake the ground As vic - t'ry fills the air.

CHORUS

Strongly marked

Our Al - ma Ma - ter's gold - en name Shall ring for ev - er-

more. Her prais - es till e - ter - ni - ty From loy - al hearts shall

The Straw Hat Band

California (The Drinking Song)

Music from central section of Air: "Rambled," with various additions
Lyrics by Various
Arrangement by Monroe Kanouse, 1957 (Incorporates corrections
by P. Elwood, J. Edginton, R. Paul and J. Vlahos)

This popular song is actually a conglomeration of five different songs that grew like Topsy over the years. The origins of some of its elements are known, but others are shrouded in mystery, and no one knows exactly how it entered the Cal song collection.

The central core of the "Drinking Song" ("California, California, the hills send back the cry. . .") is set to a contemporary vaudeville song by Bob Cole and J. Rosamund Johnson, "Oh, Didn't He Ramble." The "Drinking Song" first appeared in print in 1902 and in records in 1904. It gave birth to generations of variations (and additional sections) with no clear acknowledgment given to any single author of the lyrics. Through the years this short central core has survived, mainly through the efforts of the Band and the Glee Club, and has been wedded to additional verses and spirited tunes. The portion beginning "Sing glorious, victorious. . ." is a traditional song of conviviality, sung in many places in the United States. Although the precise origins are unclear, according to Roschelle Paul in her 1944 masters thesis, the introduction utilized here ("Oh they had a little party down at Newport . . .") may have had its genesis in a Band and Glee Club trip to Los Angeles for a Cal-UCLA game in 1939. The "Speaking Start" ("The Steward went below..."), printed below, is believed to have originated in an old Navy drinking song:

The steward went below (Shhh!)
to light the Captain's lamp. (Shhh!)
The lamp it would not light (Shhh!)
because the wick was damp. (Shhh!)
The Captain went below (Shhh!)
to kick the steward's . . . . . (Shhh!)
"Fire it up, you son-of-a bitch,
you're under the Golden Gate of .
California, California [etc.]

The California Drinking Song is included as an historical reference. Currently, the University collaborates on multiple efforts to shift the college drinking culture and address problems as serious issues rather than a harmless "rite of passage". The words of this song should not be construed to contradict these goals and efforts. Neither the University of California, the California Alumni Association nor the UC Class of 1957 intends that publication condones the improper use of alcohol.

California (The Drinking Song)

Arranged by
M. KANOUSE 1957

a cappella

Oh, they had a lit - tle par - ty down at New - port: There was
had to car - ry Har - ry to the fer - ry, And the

Har - ry, there was Lar - ry, there was Grace. Oh, they had a lit - tle par - ty down at
fer - ry car - ried Har - ry to the shore. And the rea - son that they had to car - ry

New port, And they had to car - ry Har - ry from the place. Oh, they
Har - ry to the fer - ry was that Har - ry could - n't car - ry a - ny____

more. For Cal - i - for - nia, Cal - i - for - nia, The

hills send back the cry, "We're out to do or die For Cal - i -

for - nia, Cal - i - for - nia!" We'll win the game or know the rea - son

why! And when the game is o - ver we will buy a keg of booze, And we'll

drink to Cal - i - for - nia till we wob - ble in our shoes. So drink, tra la la,

drink, tra la la, Drink, drank, drunk last night, Drunk the night be-fore,

Gon-na get drunk to-night like I nev-er got drunk be-fore, And when I'm drunk I'm as

hap - py as can be, For I am a mem - ber of the Souse fam - i - ly. Now the

Souse fam - i - ly is the best fam - i - ly That ev - er came o - ver from

old Ger - ma-ny. There's the high - land Dutch, and the low - land Dutch, The

God-damn Dutch!

Rot-ter-dam Dutch and the I - rish! Sing glo - ri-ous, vic - to - ri-ous!

One keg o' beer for the four____ of us. Sing "Glo - ry be to God that there

are no more of us, For one of us could drink it all a - lone, damn near!"

slower

Here's to the I - rish, Dead drunk! The luck - y stiffs!

Roll On

Music by Paul Yoder
Lyrics by David Mandel, 1965
Arrangement by Roschelle Paul, 1942

The music by professional composer Paul Yoder was actually part of a larger piece, "Massed Band Special," written for a 1961 Cal High School Band Day. "Roll On" was actually the "fight song" portion of the larger piece that also had an "Alma Mater" section so as to combine in one piece a fight song and an alma mater hymn. As was the case with the "California Band March," the lyrics for "Roll On" resulted from a competition within the Band, won by Band member David Mandel. According to the Cal Band website, "Roll On" became associated with the frolic of "pantsing." In the 1960s, the Band, apparently tiring of the repeated singing of the song by one of its members, divested him of his trousers, chanting the song during the process. "Pantsing" as a method of group punishment for misbehavior during marching rehearsals had been traditional with the Band for an unknown period of time, and was generally concluded by placing the purloined clothing in some public place, forcing the victim to endure the embarrassment of retrieval.

The Golden Overtones

Roll On

Lyrics by
DAVID MANDEL 1965

Music by
PAUL YODER

Roll on, you Gold - en Bear, _____ For vic - to - ry _____ is in the air, _____ For Cal - i - for - nia's fame we'll be win - ning the game _____ and for al - ma ma - ter fair. _____ So roll on, you Gold - en Bear. ____

Our loy - al band is al - ways there.

We look to thee, might - y "C,"

For Cal - i - for - nia's vic - to - ry. So

1.

2.

vic - to - ry.

Make Way For The Bear

Music by Ted E. Haley, 1915
Lyrics by Ted E. Haley, 1915
Arrangement by Roschelle Paul, 1942

"Make Way for the Bear" was written in 1965 by Ted Haley to commemorate the fiftieth anniversary of his class of 1915. This is the same Ted Haley who wrote the well-known and much loved "Stanford Jonah," the winner of the 1914 *Daily Cal* song contest. In 1966, the Cal Band included the song in its "Spirit of Cal" recording. Generally, the Band plays only the trio section, not the introduction.

Make Way For The Bear

Words and Music by
TED HALEY '15

long for Cal - i - for - nia, _____ we stride be - side the fight - ing Bear. Shout - ing loud the chal - lenge of our bat - tle cry, _____ As high a - cross the sky _____ our ban - ners proud - ly fly - ing on for Cal - i - for - nia. Rolls the tide, stand a-side, have a care! _____ For in a

might - y throng we swing a - long, 'Neath Blue and Gold so

fair, and march to vic - t'ry. _____ Make way for the

1. Bear. _____ March-ing a -   2. Bear.   Hey! Hey! We're bound for

vic - to - ry.   Make way for the   Bear! _____

Palms Of Victory

Music from Air: "Happy Days in Dixie" by Kerry Mills ("Springtime in Dixieland")
Lyrics by Stuart L. Rawlings, 1897
Arrangement by Roschelle Paul, 1942

In 1896, after the usual singing and improvising while gathered around a keg of beer, Stuart L. Rawlings created the Cal song's words to the two step, "Happy Days in Dixie" (also called "Springtime in Dixieland"). Kerry Mills, the composer, was a member of the University of Michigan faculty in 1892-93, and a famed ragtime composer writing such tunes as "Red Wing," "Meet Me in St. Louis" and "Georgia Camp Meeting." According to "Brick" Morse, the *Daily Cal* had offered a $5.00 prize for a new Cal song, and, urged on by his Phi Gamma Delta fraternity brothers, Rawlings submitted his song . . . and won. He promptly converted his winnings into another keg of beer.

"Palms of Victory" is one of the first football songs dealing with the Stanford-California rivalry, but, sad to say, at the first two Big Games when the band enthusiastically played it, California lost. After the loss of a game in the 1930s, during which the song was played, the Band became superstitious and for almost two years refused to play it. In the late 1930s the Glee Club revived it and included it in its medley of Cal songs. However, the tradition of playing the song only after a Cal win became entrenched, and currently it is played by the Band after Cal victories. Some blame California's loss of the 1992 Big Game to the fact that the Band was coaxed into playing "Palms of Victory" at alumni parties on the eve of Big Game. On the other hand, it was reportedly played at at least one Alumni party on the eve of the 1982 Big Game — the game of "The Play," the legendary last second five lateral kickoff return for the touchdown that won the game.

Palms of Victory

Words by
S. L. RAWLINGS '97

AIR: Happy Days in Dixieland

Very Lively

What will we do to the Stan-ford-ites On that great day?
How do you think we'll_ feel that night? Any-thing but cross!

We'll cel - e-brate them on that night Aft - er we play!
What - 'll the red - shirts have to say Aft - er their loss?

We now de - clare our hoo - doo's gone, Vic - tory is here!
Fill then a bump - er to the brim, For we have won!

Hit 'em a - gain, boys! Hit 'em a - gain, boys, hard - er!
Do it a - gain, boys! Do it a - gain, boys, oft - en!

CHORUS

Palms of vic - tory, Palms of glo - ry, Palms of vic - tory

we shall win! For Cal - i - Cal - i - for - nia, Palms of vic - tory,

Palms of glo - ry. Palms of vic - tory we shall win.

California Triumph

Music by Hiro Hiraiwa, 2004
Lyrics by Aaron Alcala-Mosley, 2005

"California Triumph" is the newest Cal song to become part of the Cal Band repertoire, the first to be added since "Cal Band March" in 1978. It was the result of a Spring, 2004 Band competition for a new spirit song. Hiraiwa, a four-year trombone player with the Band, won the music competition over fifteen entries from all over the United States. Since his submission did not include lyrics, another competition was held that Fall, and the entry of Alcala-Mosley, a fifth year percussion player was the winner.

California Triumph

Lyrics by
Aaron Alcala-Mosley 2005

Music by
Hiro Hiraiwa 2004

voi - ces;___ fly the ban - ner;___ from a dis - tance all they shall see___ will be the

sym - bol___ of Cal - i - for - nia's Tri - umph, ris - ing to Vic - to - ry!___

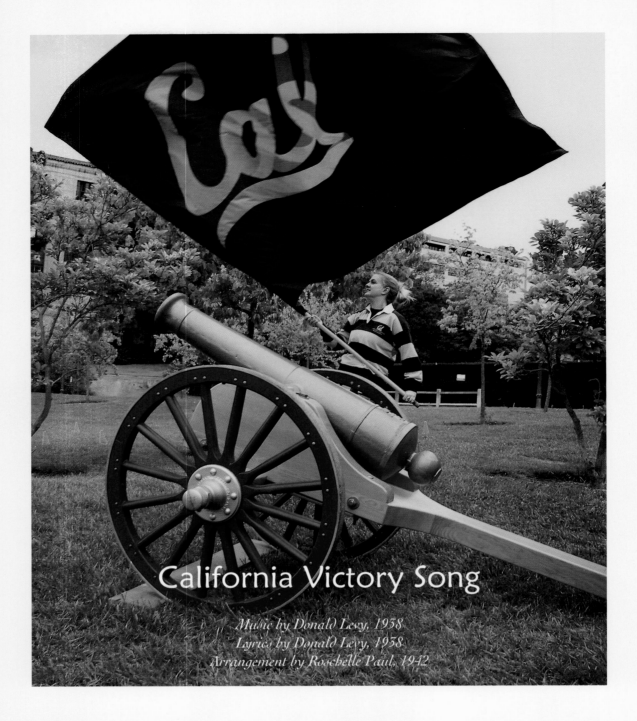

California Victory Song

Music by Donald Levy, 1938
Lyrics by Donald Levy, 1938
Arrangement by Roschelle Paul, 1942

"California Victory Song" was sung by the "Brick" Morse Collegians in the late 1930s. Although it has not been sung much since, and has not been a part of the contemporary Cal Band repertoire, it is included in this song book for historical purposes as one of the last *Daily Cal* competition prize winners of the 1930s.

The genesis of the "Collegians" sounds a rather sad note in the history of the California song tradition, for it signaled the end of Brick Morse's association with the Cal Glee Club. Morse had been the director of the Glee Club since his graduation in 1896. But in 1926, after serving in that position for 30 years, he was forced out by the A.S.U.C. Excutive Committee which refused to support a planned European Glee Club tour and asked for his resignation unless he agreed to confine the Glee Club's repertoire to "classical" music, which he refused to do. The Glee Club's program theretofore was a lively one, incorporating popular music, jazz, and vaudeville type acts. Apparently, this was deemed by some in the University administration and the A.S.U.C. Executive Committee to be inappropriate for a Cal student organization. There was also some rather oblique suggestion in articles, editorials and letters to the editor in contemporary editions of the *Daily Cal* that the deportment of Glee Club members on prior tours was less than sedate.

In an emotional speech after a "final" Glee Club rendition of Morse's "Hail to California" at Stiles Hall, Morse announced that "I have given one leg for the Varsity football team, and I am ready and willing to give the other to the Glee Club." (Morse had suffered a somewhat crippling leg injury during his football career at Cal.) With that statement, he left the room, no longer to be the Glee Club's director. The entirety of the Varsity and freshman Glee Club (save one member, the manager) resigned en masse and joined the new, off-campus "Collegians," formed by Morse to continue the kind of programming that the Glee club had been performing.

While these events struck a rather discordant note at the time, history has firmly entrenched Morse as one of the foremost contributors to the Cal song heritage.

California Victory Song

Words and Music by
DONALD LEVY '38

We'll give a rous - ing cheer our team is here,____
We're gon - na fight, fight, fight, for vic - to - ry,____

____ To fight for Cal - i - for - nia fame, We're gon - na
____ We'll give a grand old Os - ki roar, We're gon - na

hit that line we're gon - na shine,____ Our Gold - en
cheer, cheer, cheer, our Var - si - ty,____ As they go

Bear will win this game, They say there's great a -
rol - lin' up that score, As we fight on, on,

larm down on the farm,_____ Our bat - tle cry rings

on, it won't be long,_____ Be - fore our team will

o - ver head,_____ Oh! the Car - di - nals_____ be -

break a - way,_____ And we'll win an - oth - er

1.

ware boys, And down with the Stan - ford Red._____

2.

vic - tory_____ For the Gol - den Bear to - day._____

One More River

Music from Air: "Noah's Ark"
Lyrics by unknown authors

This song, as played by the Cal Band, is actually a combination of two songs. The portion of "One More River" used here was the Junior Class entrance music at rallies in the 1920s as juniors had "one more river to cross" (their senior year), but its origins as a Cal song are obscure. According to Marv Levy, former Cal and later professional football coach with the Buffalo Bills (and a history Ph.D. as well), it was originally a British Army song. This was confirmed by a number of World War I band records. Levy sang the song and had his Cal players sing the chorus as a motivational inspiration.

Since the 1950s, the original song, combined with an arrangement by Larry Austin of an old ribald tune (not reproduced here but delicately referred to as "OBR"), has been part of the Cal Band's exit march through the North Tunnel of Memorial Stadium after football games. Back in the Pappy Waldorf days of the late 1940s and early 1950s, the Band would play the "One More River" section of the song while exiting through the crowds in the North Tunnel on the way to hear Coach Waldorf's balcony speech. Then, after several repetitions during the slow progress through the tunnel, the Band would launch into the "OBR" section upon reaching the other end. In more recent times, the Band has instead crossed the field after football games to play a post-game concert for the fans remaining in the stands, and then so quickly exits through the now empty North Tunnel that the "OBR" section was written into the music to immediately follow the "One More River" section. While the Band has a cleansed version of the lyrics to the "OBR" section of the song, only the chorus part of the song printed here is generally known to and sung by students and alumni.

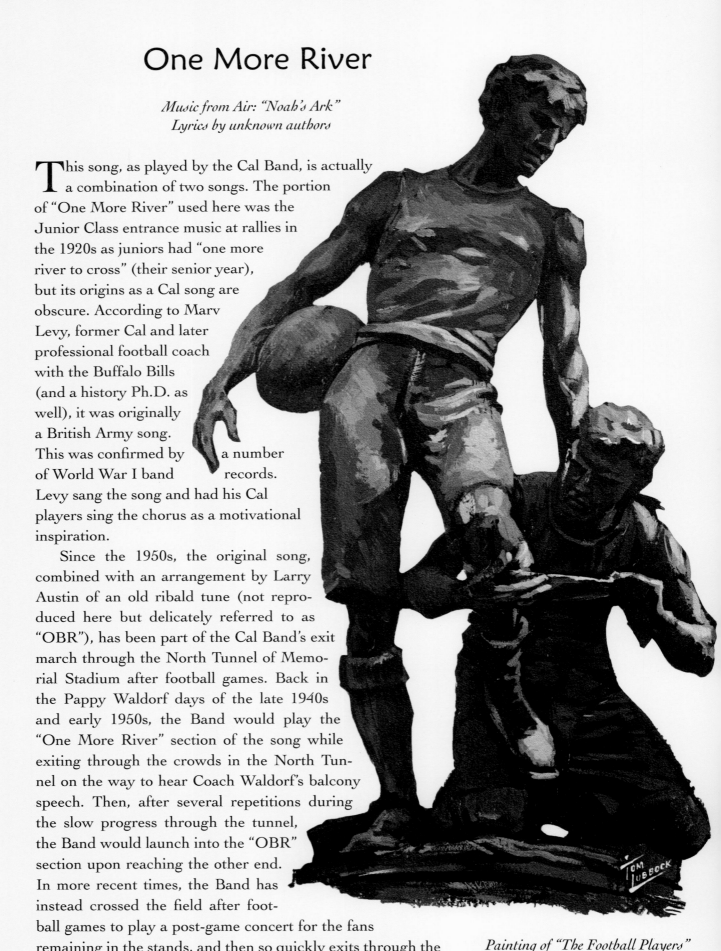

Painting of "The Football Players"
(sculpture by Douglas Tilden)

One More River

TRADITIONAL

AIR: Noah's Ark

Instrumental

CHORUS

One   more   riv - er,   One   more riv - er to   cross,

One   more   riv - er,   One   more riv - er to   cross._____

California Indian Song

Music by H. W. Bingham, 1906
Lyrics by H. W. Bingham, 1906

Harold W. Bingham wrote the "California Indian Song" long before Stanford officially adopted the name "Indians" as its team's mascot. It appears in a Cal song book as early as 1913. A bit of history places this song in context:

Until 1930, Stanford's teams had no "mascot." While Stanford students originally voted for gold as the school's official color, a later student vote favored cardinal. After the first Big Game in 1891, the newspapers picked up the cardinal color of the Stanford team and used the word in their stories. (White was added as a second color in the 1940s.) In 1930, the "Indian" nickname, which had already been used, was officially adopted. It remained the name of the Stanford mascot until 1972, and for decades Harry Delmar "Timm" Williams (known as "Prince Lightfoot"), a member of the Yurok tribe, would, in Native American costume, lead the Stanford band onto the field with a native dance. In 1972, because of increased sensitivity to issues of culture and heritage, and responding to protests from Native American students and supporters, Stanford dropped the use of "Indians" for its athletic teams. While an initial student vote in 1972 favored restoration of the name, a second vote in 1975 was resoundingly against it. Other proposed names were put to vote that year — e.g., Robber Barons, Sequoias, Cardinals, Railroaders, Spikes and Huns — but none was adopted. An effort in 1978 to adopt the name "Griffins" also failed. From 1972 until 1981, Stanford's teams were known as the "Cardinals." As the reference was to the color and not the bird, then Stanford President Donald Kennedy declared in 1981 that Stanford's teams would be called "The Cardinal." The Tree, an invention of the Stanford band, is not an official mascot.

As the Cal Band still plays the music to the "California Indian Song," it has been included in this song book. The lyrics, with their references to scalping, tomahawks and the like, are no longer sung. They have not been included in this song book for the much same reason that the name "Indians" was dropped by Stanford in 1972.

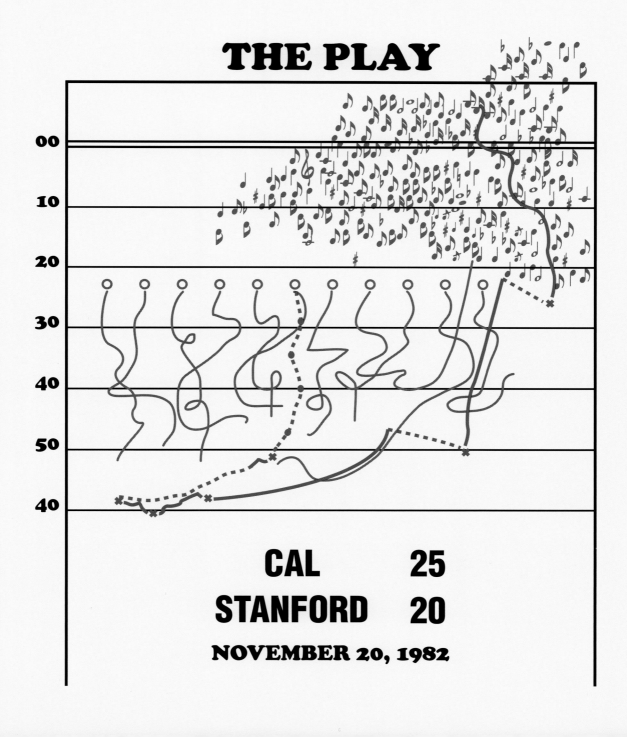

THE PLAY

CAL   **25**
STANFORD   **20**
NOVEMBER 20, 1982

California Indian Song

Words and Music by
H. W. Bingham, 1906

CHORUS

All Hail! Blue And Gold

Music by Harold W. Bingham, 1906
Lyrics by Harold W. Bingham, 1906
Arrangement by Albert Elkus, 1906

Harold W. Bingham, a prolific writer of Cal songs, wrote the words and the music to "All Hail! Blue and Gold" in 1905. Prior to that time, Cal had no Alma Mater, but once introduced and popularized by the Glee Club and a quartet called the "Budweiser Quartet" (Bingham being a member of both), "All Hail" was quickly adopted by the student body as the University's first Alma Mater hymn.

It was sung at the conclusion of all formal gatherings, meetings and athletic meets. The cry "Stick around for 'All Hail'" quickly became part of the campus vocabulary. To this day, although Brick Morse's "Hail to California" has threatened to replace it in popularity, "All Hail" is still played at the conclusion of Cal athletic events, but, sadly, nowadays most students no longer "stick around" to sing it. Perhaps this song book will serve to revitalize the tradition.

All Hail! Blue and Gold

Arranged by
ALBERT ELKUS '06

Words and Music by
HAROLD BINGHAM '06

Moderate, not too slow

All hail! Blue and Gold, Thy col - ors un - fold O'er
All hail! Blue and Gold, To thee we shall cling; O'er

loy - al Cal - i - for - nians, Whose hearts are strong and
gold - en fields of pop - pies, Thy prais - es we will

bold. All hail! Blue and Gold, Thy strength ne'er shall
sing. All hail! Blue and Gold, On breez - es ye

fail; For thee we'll die! All hail! All hail!
sail; Thy sight we love! All hail! All hail!

PHOTO AND ART CREDITS

viii, Reprinted from *California Pilgrimage,* Robert and Carol Sibley, 1952

4, Reprinted from *The University of California, A Pictorial History,* Albert G. Pickerell and May Dornin, 1968

6, © Dana Davis (www.danadavisphoto.com)

8, The Bancroft Library

9, The Bancroft Library

12, Reprinted from *The Pride of California,* Cal Band History Committee, 1993

14, Courtesy of Rally Committee

15 (top), © Tom Lubbock, pen and ink

15 (bottom), Courtesy of Cal Spirit Groups

18-19, Courtesy of Cal Band

19 (top and middle), The Bancroft Library

22, © Mike Wondolowski

23 (top), © Mike Wondolowski

23 (bottom), Courtesy of Cal Spirit Groups

28, The Bancroft Library

29, The Bancroft Library

34, © Barry Evans

36, © Takane Eshima

38, Courtesy of N.H. (Dan) Cheatham

42, The Bancroft Library

43, Courtesy of N.H. (Dan) Cheatham

48, Reprinted from *The Pride of California,* Cal Band History Committee, 1993

49 (top), Courtesy of Cal Spirit Groups

49 (bottom), Courtesy of California Golden Overtones

52, Courtesy of University of California Sports Information, reprinted from *100 Years of Blue & Gold,* Nick Peters

56, Courtesy of N.H. (Dan) Cheatham

57 (top and bottom), © Tom Lubbock, pen and ink

57 (middle), Courtesy of Cal Spirit Groups

60, Courtesy of Cal Spirit Groups

61, Courtesy of N.H. (Dan) Cheatham

64, Courtesy of N.H. (Dan) Cheatham

65, © Mike Wondolowski

68, © Tom Lubbock, acrylic painting

70, © Robert Stinnett

71, © Paul Behrend

74, Photograph of Professor Chiura Obata painting, courtesy of Chancellor and Mrs. Robert Birgeneau

Back cover, © Takane Eshima

INDEX TO FIRST LINES [*]

---

[*]   Where the Chorus of a song may be more familiar than the Introduction or the second verse more familiar than the first, the first lines of both are set forth.